what I wish for you
simple wisdom for a happy life

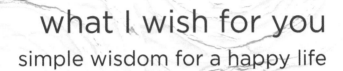

patti digh

skirt!

Guilford, Connecticut
An imprint of Globe Pequot Press

skirt!® is an attitude . . . spirited, independent, outspoken, serious, playful and irreverent, sometimes controversial, always passionate.

Design by Diana Nuhn
Layout by Maggie Peterson

Library of Congress Cataloging-in-Publication Data is available on file.

ISBN 978-0-7627-7062-5

Printed in China

10 9 8 7 6 5 4 3 2 1

For Emma and Tess:

What I wish for you is happiness.
That is all.

And that is everything.

"Be happy.
It's one way
of being wise."
—*Colette*

Contents

The line at the edge of seeing is either a horizon
or a boundary — ix

CHAPTER 1. Remember who you are: ***be you*** — 1

CHAPTER 2. Know what matters most: ***be passionate*** — 27

CHAPTER 3. Make peace with time: ***be present*** — 49

CHAPTER 4. Let go of certainty: ***be unsure*** — 69

CHAPTER 5. Learn something every day: ***be curious*** — 85

CHAPTER 6. Open up your hand: ***be free*** — 115

It's in your hands — 137

Artists & writers — 140

Gratitudes — 142

About the author — 144

—*contributed by Kim Mailhot*

The line at the edge of seeing is either a horizon or a boundary

I watched my brother and sister-in-law on a beach a few years ago as they stood at the edge of the world, a point of land jutting into ocean water, the sun setting and making that sky I like so much, blue-gray and white tinged with pink, flinging their only son—my favorite nephew—into that horizon as he married, standing with his bride inside a heart carved of sand, strewn with flower petals and shells, the tide reminding me of forces much larger into which all this is set, those gravitational urges that we all feel on a smaller scale than the earth, the sun, and the moon.

As I looked out into the sea, I realized that the line at the edge of seeing is either a horizon or a boundary, depending on your perspective. It either keeps moving, sweeping you with it to new parts of the globe inside you, or it doesn't. In such vast travel, a compass is vital.

At that moment, I felt my heart catch as I watched my daughter Emma, barefoot in her sundress and newly dyed pink-and-black hair and arms festooned with black bracelets, one made of tire rubber and bottle caps, the other with a silver rectangle that read "redefine normal," watching the wedding. She was standing on the edge of the sea and on the eve of turning fifteen in a few days, readying herself for a visit to a college on our way home from the beach, a place in which she would try to imagine herself walking and laughing and creating art and living and eating Cheerios and microwave macaroni and cheese.

What will that moment be like when I turn her over to the world, wait for a good wind, and fling her into the horizon to do her own living, her own work in the world, like a kite with a long tail? My heart exploded and then started reconfiguring itself—with changes—inside my chest.

I turned from the wedding to see Emma's little sister, Tess, skipping in the water, going farther out as her beloved daddy stood by at a distance to allow for both safety and freedom, picking up sand and throwing it. She wiped her sandy hands on her pretty party dress, poking at sea foam with sticks, reveling in her first visit to the ocean. She was still reeling from our earlier swim in this magnificent huge wavy pool, those white crests crashing over her, knocking us both down, me desperate to hold her head above the wave and not lose her to the current, but getting thrown down myself, scraping my free hand on the hard bottom of the sea, and feeling the waves carry my red plastic Lafont eyeglasses with their happy and significant progressive bifocal lenses away from me.

My panic at losing those glasses is but a drop compared with my panic at losing them, my precious daughters. In my head I see the waves crashing, that kite string snapping, but also the compass always pointing—not north, but home.

And now, the time has come. My older daughter, Emma, grew up in the pages of my blog, *37days*. As she prepared to graduate from high school and fly away, a prospect that sent my fast-beating heart beating faster, I wanted to prepare her, shore up her innate sense of self with some thoughts from outside her own experience. And so I reached out to readers of *37days* to gather wisdom from the far corners of the earth to guide Emma as she traded one space for another, as she ventured into the world—still connected but in a vastly different way. What would you say to her? Or to your own seventeen-year-old self?, I asked. What thoughts would you ask her to consider? What would you have be her compass?

What came pouring in amazed me, touched me, made me think about my own life. Could I have known those things at seventeen, even if someone told me? Perhaps not. Probably not. Life's lessons are less to be put on like a shawl or a jacket than they are to be surfaced from somewhere deep inside us where disappointment and regret and hurt live. But the depth and breadth and sheer love in those messages moved me deeply. And I think they'll touch your heart, too. And the heart of a young graduate, perhaps, who one day when you least expect it will pick up this book and know. He or she will recognize the truth in them. Someday. And so might women on the verge of a new life, or corporate executives finally stopping to take a breath and asking themselves, at last, "Is this all there is, these meetings and spreadsheets and long waits in airports?"

The hundreds of essays I received from readers were beautiful expressions of the wellsprings of wisdom we all possess, when we sit still long enough to access that inner voice, the one that gets lost in cramming for exams or making lunch sandwiches without crusts for second graders or creating agendas for board meetings. We are wise enough, each of us, at every age. Wise enough. If only we find the wisdom to realize that, and to bring that wisdom out into the world, as these writers have done. I could have sought advice from celebrities named Johnny Depp or famous poets named Billy Collins or people who have climbed Mount Everest barefoot or sailed solo across the Atlantic or invented tomato-and-lettuce sandwiches. But I wanted to uncover the wisdom we all possess, not that attributed greater power simply because of who said it and what they had done. We have all climbed our own mountains and written our own poems with our lives, and we're all sailing solo across vast oceans every single day, aren't we?

There is a deep humanity in these simple expressions of wisdom—one you possess as well. Tap into that as you read. If you are buying this book for a recent graduate, there might be some messages in here for you, too. Add your own thoughts in the margins and give this book to someone in transition who might sit with it as he rides the train to a job he doesn't love, to someone who feels like a flight risk in long business meetings, to someone as she sits in her dorm room for the first evening alone without you, or to someone teetering on the brink of divorce, not knowing what sun will rise the next morning, if any.

For people in transition, I wanted these essays to be seen simply as things to consider, not as prescriptions or rules or chains. There is no rocket science here because, truthfully, the formula for a happy life is simple, really. Very, very simple. And yet, when we look for it too earnestly, it eludes us: "If you observe a really happy man," writes W. Beran Wolfe, "you will find him building a boat, writing a symphony, educating his son, growing double dahlias in his garden, or looking for dinosaur eggs in the Gobi desert. He will not be searching for happiness as if it were a collar button that has rolled under the radiator."

As Thornton Wilder has said, "My advice to you is not to inquire why or whither, but just enjoy your ice cream while it's on your plate." So these are just beautifully simple things to consider, for those venturing forth in the world for the first time, and for the rest of us, the ones still venturing.

All I want to say to you is just consider this.

—*contributed by Susie Riley*

CHAPTER 1

Remember who you are: *be you*

—contributed by Hollis G. Fouts

This is an essay for parents and other caring adults—and for the children and young people they love. And for the rest of us at any age who are trying to remember who we are, too. If you've bought this book for a young graduate, read this essay before giving the book to him or her. If you've received this book as a graduation present, pay particular attention to the italicized parenthetical phrases. The non-italicized bits will have metaphoric, abstract meaning at the moment, and more concrete meaning later in your life, perhaps.

Emma just picked where she will go to college in the fall. COLLEGE. DID YOU HEAR THAT? MY TINY LITTLE LOVE BABY IS GOING TO COLLEGE. Step back and let me breathe here for a moment. Suddenly I feel very warm and shaky. *(Your parents are feeling warm and shaky, too. Be as kind as possible on move-in weekend.)*

I wanted her to go to a small school because that's what I did; the one she picked has 30,000 students. I wanted her to consider my alma mater because that's what I did; it was her last choice. I wanted a small campus environment for her because that's what I had; she is going to the largest school she applied to, a huge institution in the midst of a large city. I went to a small Quaker college. She will join the 300-member marching band at a very large state university, having chosen the tuba and sousaphone rather than the nice quiet portable flute I suggested when she was in the sixth grade. I wished for a Harvard or a Stanford or one of the beautifully pristine little private colleges that offered her full scholarships; she wished for a school that fulfilled her three criteria: computer animation courses, a marching band, and an equestrian program. It is hard to find a place with all three, but she did. She knows so much more about what she wants and who she is than I did at her age. At almost any age. Okay, at every age. *(Seriously, we adults mean well. We just can't help ourselves.)*

This is all really good information for me, a handy reminder: She is not me. *(You are not your parents.)*

Repeat that after me: She is not me. *(You are not your parents. And evolution is sometimes messy because parents like to share wisdom that fits their own life, and not necessarily yours. This is really just part of their job description. Smile graciously and take notes and make poetry of all those notes and file them away, then take them out late one night when you're in your fifties and smile and say a silent thanks.)*

She is not even an undeveloped youth version of me. This is useful information to remember in the case of partners, spouses, children, coworkers, and bosses, even: She is not me. She will not grow up to be me. *(You may look shockingly like your parents as you age—it might be important to be prepared for that. But you won't grow up to be them.)* Knowing that is important. In fact, let's put that at the head of the list:

Know they aren't you. Just because you are older than your children doesn't make you the expert in what they want or need. Listen to them before trying to convince them that your path is the best path. It was for you. Not necessarily for them. Sure, you gave birth to her and fed her organic free-trade vegetables with a wee curve-handled spoon and dressed her in adorable tiny sailor suits and kept her safe for all these years and people all said that "she looks just like you!"—yet she ALL ALONG was an independent being. ALL ALONG. From the moment she popped out into the world. What you gained by being one of only eight slightly hung-over freshmen studying the imagery of Henry James in Lee Johnson's office in the English Department at Guilford College isn't what she needs or wants. It truly isn't. Watch other people for clues about who THEY are, not just for clues about how much they are or are not like YOU. *(Your parents are also individual human beings with whole lives outside of being parents—try to step beyond the roles and see them as real people, even with all their irritating habits like pushing your hair out of your eyes and looking at their watch when you say you're going out and it is past 10:00 p.m.)*

See them right now. Too many of us look at small children as they grow and wonder, "What will they be when they grow up?" rather than pondering, "Who are they now?" They are fully human at even the tiniest of ages. We do a disservice to our children by the anticipation with which we wait for them to emerge. They have emerged. They are themselves, with their own needs and dreams and fears. Sure, teens have brains that aren't fully developed, and for that reason our job is to keep them safe. But not to discount them. Don't anticipate what they will be; explore who they are now. Pay attention to the "now" as much as (and maybe more than) the "future." *(Be worthy of respect at every age, whether or not it is given.)*

Provide them with options. I have always believed I could do anything. My parents said I could. (There is a downside to that, also, if it results in the feeling that you must.) I didn't come from wealthy parents—my father was a barber. It wasn't money that would open doors for me, it was the belief that there were no boundaries. Did I want to go to Sri Lanka in high school as an exchange student, to live in a country I had never heard of? Yes, let's find a way to do that. Do I want to study trapeze with Sam Keen? Yes, let's write the man a letter and maybe he will say yes. (He did! He did!) My job for Emma— and for Tess—is to open a big wide door to a big wide world. One that is realistic and hugely imaginative and wild and wondrous at the same time. You want to know why the author of your first-grade reading book always puts a pair of spectacles in every painting? Let's find him (in London) and call him up and ask. Make possibilities sparkle regardless of circumstance. Curiosity is not just for the wealthy. *(Boredom has no place on the planet. Ask more questions than you think polite. It's okay.)*

Just follow their lead. I met with Emma's second-grade teacher once. "I'm really worried about Emma," I said. "She is so unnaturally fearful. She is terrified of speaking in class. The book report you assigned her is a source of great, immense anxiety for her. I'm worried about her." "Tell me about yourself at her age," the wise teacher asked. And so I waxed poetic about being on the student council and in school plays as Johnny Appleseed. She let me talk and talk. "Well," she said after a while. "That's your personality and this is hers." Stop trying to make other people into a mini me. *(And stop trying to be a mini me of anyone else. Anyone.)*

Don't "fix" their story. People change. Children evolve. So do adults. My story of Emma for a long time was that she was shy (see above). A summer at camp showed me the ways in which I was pigeonholing her into a story that no longer fit her. When I took another look, I saw the slight girl who carries a heavy sousaphone during marching band season as section leader, who rides a retro scooter around town, who creates her own graphic novel for her senior project, who chooses the huge college. Listen to the story you tell of others. Be willing to change it. *(Listen to the story you've been told about yourself. Be willing to shed it.)*

Offer help, step back. Applying for college is fundamentally different now. No longer are there big packages of applications on the dining room table—no. It's almost all done online. Emma handled her applications herself. "Don't you want help doing the essays?" both John and I asked, thinking we needed to step in and give her advice. "No," she said, "I've already submitted them." "What if there are grammatical errors in them?" John asked me later. "Then I guess there are grammatical errors in them," I said. "And she will either get in or she won't because of them, but it will be her own process." Your job is not to save other people, AS TEMPTING AS THAT MIGHT BE. Support, not save. This is easy when the stakes are small; the true test is when the stakes feel big. *(Know when to ask for* *help, but mainly take on the task of living yourself. Life is a verb, after all, to be grabbed hold of and lived out loud.)*

Let learning be hot. When Emma was eleven and in the fifth grade, we moved to Asheville the November after school had started. It was a tough move to a whole new place and school, not helped by the fact that she now had for a teacher the most difficult person I'd ever encountered in that role. We celebrated the end of that school year with an "I survived Mrs. _____" cake and certificate, it was so bad. "You should move her into another classroom," many people said at the time. Unless there is undeniable psychological or physical danger, I don't socially engineer life for my children, as much as I might be tempted to. Will Emma face difficult people in her life? Yes. Will navigating them be easier because she had to navigate Mrs. _____? I hope so, I think so. Was it tremendously difficult not to step in and demand a change? You bet it was. If I felt at any time she was in real danger, I would have stepped in. But having a difficult time and being in danger are two different things. Learning comes at the edges. Take away the edges and you take away the learning. *(Don't ask other people to save you, but know when to ask for support. Everything is free data, even the mean, uncomfortable, unfair bits.)*

Lower the high bar. I am an overachiever of the highest order. I admit that. I love to learn and do and see if I can achieve something—not so much for the achievement, but for the thrill of the process. Halloween costumes? Homemade. It's just way more fun. Perfectionism? You bet. I hate misspellings (THE

WORD *ACCOMMODATION* HAS TWO *C*'s AND TWO *M*'s, people!). And yet I'm trying to lower my own bar as I've lowered the bar for Emma and Tess. So many parents fret over the success of their children—did they get into AP classes, the National Honor Society? Not of interest to her. Let it go. Let it go. It's not that you have a bigger and better perspective on what matters—you have YOUR perspective (and, frankly, it's likely old school). Sometimes it helps, and often it doesn't. Sometimes you are trying to fix what was missing in your own childhood, or trying to re-create it. But wait: This is a whole new child.

Frankly, I have a very low bar when it comes to my children—it's not that I don't want them to be happy and successful, whatever that means to them. I do. I desperately do, like most parents. But I love them whether they are reaching their potential or not. My bar? Keep them alive. Do whatever it takes to keep them alive. Just keep them alive. That's it. That's a lot, and sometimes we know that isn't possible, we can't save them—but we must do what we can. Anything above that? Gravy, pure gravy. The kid's room is a mess? Close the door. He still comes home at night and somehow sleeps in there. Ease up there, cowboy. Let people know you love them no matter what. And step in when they are in real danger. *(Pick your battles wisely. Choose your own definition of happy.)*

Celebrate with wild abandon. Emma applied to five colleges and got in all five. Sure enough, a "Five for Five" cake arrived at the dinner table. She made her college decision? I immediately ordered sweatshirts for the whole family with that school's logo emblazoned on them. Celebrate way more than needed. Daily even. *(Endure celebrations even when embarrassed by them. Perhaps one day you'll be embarrassing children of your own. It is, after all, an art form.)*

Parenting is an exercise in letting go. So is living. Be who you are, and let others be their own precious selves, connected to you like the people in Virginia Woolf's *Mrs. Dalloway*, tenuous and invisible threads linking her to people all over London. Those threads can both buoy and strangle you. Be you. In deep, wondrous, hot, and chaotic relation to others, but not in the shadow of them.

> *The essays in this chapter speak deeply to me in my fifties, having just now become who I am. Perhaps I am a slow learner, or perhaps there is a certain rhythm to being fully who we are, like the ripening figs in my backyard that won't sweeten before their time. These essays say these things I believe my daughters knew more clearly in their early years than I have ever known: You are enough just as you are. Sure, there will be people who try to say you aren't, that you need to color, straighten, lighten, lose, emulate. Don't listen to them. Just show up fully human, fully beautifully flawed and imperfect and chaotic and hot and cold and truly beautiful. Because even if you have spinach caught between your front teeth, you have a friend who will tell you so, and it doesn't matter anyway because you are also peculiarly beautiful with spinach between your teeth.*

—contributed by Allison Graham

You are already who you are going to be

One springtime afternoon when my son was in the seventh grade, the guidance counselors visited his sixth-period class. He was not at all prepared for what they asked him to do.

He came home sullen and with a backpack full of booklets with small print describing every job you could possibly imagine: Nuclear Physicist. Landscape Architect. Urinal Attendant.

"It's time," he said.

"For what?" I asked.

"The guidance counselors told us it's time to decide what we are going to be. They are coming back tomorrow for answers."

He spread out the materials. Pet Food Tester. Teacher. Nurse. Mechanic. "Am I 'geared toward the helping professions'? Do I need a structured work environment? Would I do best working outdoors? Am I a 'people person'? Do they want me to think about what I like to do now when I am twelve or later when I have to work?"

For a kid who was not once overwhelmed with his homework assignments (he just never did them), this one seemed to be very different. He sat at the kitchen table for a long time.

The next morning we talked about it.

"You okay, babe?"

"Yeah. I've got it. I figured out what I want to be when I grow up."

"You have?"

With his braces full of powdered sugar doughnuts, he said, "Dunk tank clown."

"Is that seasonal work?"

"Probably. During the colder months I want to be the innocent guy in police lineups."

And then he left for school. And he was fine. I was fine. We both knew what he was going to be when he grew up. He was going to be Buddy. Funny, smart, creative Buddy.

You, too, are already who you are going to be. Funny, smart, beautiful, talented, thoughtful, creative. Just be you.

—contributed by Amy D. McCracken

—contributed by Rebeca Price

—contributed by Kerrie Blazek

Don't shy down

I want you to use your voice. I want you to yell and scream and run and jump and use every bit of energy you have to race around the block, banging on drums and cymbals, car hoods and trunks, neighbors' doors, the bells on bikes, tree stumps, and trash cans.

I want you to be loud and fierce and wild, unable to be tamed. I want you to slip and slide, get wet in fountains and sprinklers, splash with all your might, and then get back to screaming for justice, for your mama, for another piece of pie, for a world that's being raped by ignorance and intolerance.

I want to know that every bit of power you were born with has been harnessed and is in full use so that when you need strength, you won't have to rely on your reserves. I want you dressed in liberty with a gray smile and a flaming torch.

You will meet people who will want you to shrink back so that they can step into the spotlight and claim all the warmth. Don't let them. Move forward, take the light, accept the applause, understand how brilliant you are.

People will inevitably say mean things to you or about you; don't suck those things under your skin and try to make sense of them. Bust forth, make demands, speak up, don't shy down.

—*contributed by Chi Sherman*

Tell them what you really do

Soon you will be asked the proverbial "adult" question, the question people ask when they want to make some kind of sense about who you are, when they don't know what else to say, when they want to make assumptions, judgments, and comparisons. Don't let them. Don't you dare give them a one-word job title or a prepared thirty-second elevator speech. Tell them what you *really* do and then ask them a question that will blow their hair back just as much as your answer did.

Tell them you do your best to get a good night's sleep and move your body on a regular basis. Tell them you make a mean stir-fry and on occasion a delicious dessert to celebrate a friend's birthday. Tell them you do kind things for strangers and you do French accents with flair. Tell them you still do laundry at home sometimes because you miss your parents and it gives you a decent amount of time to catch up with each other. Tell them what you do that makes your heart sing and your spirit soar.

What question should you ask them? Not "What do you *do*?" but "What do you love to do?"

—*contributed by Lisa Evans*

—*contributed by Karl Stephan*

—contributed by Jolie Guillebeau

Shake them off

Amid all the goodness and love in life, you'll encounter random anger, ridicule, insults, resentment, indifference, rudeness, moodiness, and insensitivity. When you do, please remember that most of the time, it has nothing to do with you. While we're sometimes a *target* for others' feelings, we are often not the *reason* for them. Those feelings are theirs; please don't make them yours or own them or become responsible for them. If you must own something, let it be your need to offer gentle support and love.

Even when you know these feelings have nothing to do with you—and even if you weren't the intended target—they will sometimes stick. *Shake them off.* In your mind, see yourself blowing them away and dissolving them into the air. Don't let them ruin a good shirt, a good mood, or a good friendship. And to those who sent out these feelings, offer hugs, smiles, healing thoughts, warm wishes or prayers—always positive, never negative.

—*contributed by Susie Riley*

Always trust your own heart

Love as much as you can, with your whole heart. This won't ensure that you will be loved back or that your heart won't be broken. It will only ensure that you are a loving person.

Trust that the world is wide and beautiful and holds many surprises and delights. See as much as you can. Learn how others live differently from you. Explore how they cook their food, how they love their children and one another, how they build their homes and clothe their bodies. Learn how they celebrate the important moments in their lives. Let all of this influence you. And dare to hope. Hope that this planet survives. Hope that cancer will be cured. Hope that children will stop being hurt. Hope for whatever it is that your heart holds dear.

Be a loving, trusting, hopeful person. And always trust your own heart.

—contributed by Teresa Hartley

—contributed by Cynthia N. Clack

—contributed by Linda Bannan

Never dim your light

As you launch into the world
with your own personal trajectory
seek that which makes you comfortable
even if it's not what others would choose.
Admit your mistakes with grace,
find the power in humility
as you revel in your accomplishments.
Spill kindness onto the world,
don't let forgiveness be a stranger,
know that you are loved unconditionally,
and never, ever dim your light.

—*contributed by Marilyn Maciel*

Your dream has its own heartbeat.
Listen for it.

Remember the joy you first felt when you discovered what you love to do. Find a few people who believe wholly in you and protect these relationships with all your might. Don't ask everyone you know for feedback. Creativity is subjective, and your art will find its tribe. Your dream has its own heartbeat. Listen for it.

It's a DIY world, but you can't do it alone. Build your team as wisely as you would choose typefaces or words for lyrics. Embrace your place on earth as a creative. Give thanks you were given this gift to share. Turn a deaf ear to those who say the path of art is hard. Doing something you don't love is a much harder path. Study the patterns of your mind and honor your needs for time alone to create.

Accept that not everyone will "get" what you are doing, even those close to you. If you ever doubt the value of your gift, imagine a day without sound, music, art, or design. Remember that rejections are the building blocks of success.

Don't measure your success. Your steps will often be infinitesimal.

Admire those who have walked the path you are on, and know it is a shared path. Concentrate on the square you are standing in right now. Tomorrow it will be a new one. Don't compare yourself with those you admire. Babies learning to walk aren't compared with long-distance runners. Each is on his own path to movement.

Make your evolution your priority. You grow through change. Moments of fear are often signals of change on the horizon. Listen carefully to them.

Learn to let go. You can't control how people react to you. You can only control how and what you think about yourself. Edit out those people who instill fear, doubt, or negative thinking into your world.

And remember to look back at how far you have traveled. If you only see the mountains ahead, you will forget those you have already climbed.

—*contributed by Deb Walsh*

—*contributed by Debbi Crane*

"It's not about
what you get,
it is all in
what you bring."
—*contributed by*
David Robinson

CHAPTER 2

Know what matters most: *be passionate*

—contributed by *Maxine Rothman*

everal times lately, I've gotten messages from readers or Facebook "fans" advising me that speaking out about gay rights or Islamic tolerance isn't a good idea when I'm "putting myself out there trying to sell a book." I admit to being rendered completely speechless by these messages. "If I let selling a book stand in the way of voicing my opinion on things that matter to me," I responded to one woman on Facebook, "then I am surely lost." Unfortunately she would never see that response, having de-friended me immediately after writing her message to me.

What do you care about? What matters most to you? On what topics is your voice invaluable, necessary, potent? What must you say to the world, or you will die? What do only *you* see in the way that you see it? If you don't know, seek to find what that is.

On YouTube recently, I again saw footage of Martin Luther King Jr.'s "I have a dream" speech at the Lincoln Memorial. I have found as I've made my way into adulthood in this life of mine that I share his dream. And that I have dreams of my own. Perhaps it is important to articulate our dreams, to know what matters most to us, to see how that changes over time, or doesn't. Here's my dream. You might not share my dream. What's yours?

I have a dream that we won't fool ourselves into thinking Dr. King's dream has been realized. That one day we will stand in lines all night long to find solutions to child abuse and child hunger, just like we stand in lines all night to buy iPads, and Harry Potter books, and tickets to the next Star Wars movie. I have a dream that what happened to Matthew Shepard and James Byrd and Lawrence King will never happen to anyone else, that we will never see human beings as abstractions or "whats" but always as "whos," people who are as fully textured as we are, whether they are CEOs or are homeless.

I have a dream that we will wake up and realize the discrimination we impose on our lesbian, gay, transgender, queer, and intersex friends and neighbors is immoral, that we will be as ashamed of it in twenty years as we are of the behavior of our grandparents in the 1950s when they propagated discrimination against blacks. I have a dream that no child will go hungry tonight, no child will be gang-raped in her lifetime, no child will be bullied into killing himself.

I have a dream that when we ask "how are you?" we will stop to hear the answer. That every person who is contemplating suicide will find someone to reach out to instead. I have a dream that we will protest disparities in our criminal justice system and health care system like our hair is on fire.

I have a dream that we find a way to walk toward and embrace the darkness in our lives as a rich soil for growth instead of protecting ourselves and others from it. I have a dream that children who are spirited, who have autism or Asperger's, or who are now seen as outcasts or "problems" for any reason will be recognized for the gifts they bring the world.

I have a dream that peace is as prosperous as war. That everyone who was hurt or traumatized in their childhood will get the help they need not to perpetuate that pain into another generation.

I have a dream that we will choose to be optimistic in the face of despair, and naive rather than cynical. That we will all spend a year getting to know someone who scares us, and that we will all recognize we are the storyteller and not just the listener.

I have a dream that we will find prejudice and hatred and ridicule in others not as an opportunity for prejudice and hatred and ridicule on our part, but as an occasion for learning and teaching. I have a dream that we can all learn to give up our need to be right in order to hear one another's perspectives.

I have a dream that we will recognize we are always in choice. That women will one day be able to walk to their car late at night without holding their keys in their hands like a defensive weapon. That we will find a cure for MS, CF, ALS, spinal cord injuries, and cancer. And soon.

I have a dream that white males will be allowed to cry freely without being teased about it. That my children and your children will take the best of what we offer them and leave the rest behind.

I have a dream that teachers, nurses, and artists will finally be recognized for the national treasures they are, and that teachers will make as much money as basketball players. I have a dream that education will be transformed into a system that focuses on learning, not teaching or containing or testing.

I have a dream that we will all sit quietly and very still for just ten minutes every day, that we will learn how to listen half as well as we judge, and that giving becomes our national pastime, not getting.

I have a dream that every lonely child will find a friend who loves her.

I have a dream that we can find commonality amid a glorious celebration of difference, and that we will stop confusing noticing difference with making a judgment. I have a dream that we will consider volunteering to help others less fortunate to be our birthright, not our punishment.

I have a dream that, as Henri Nouwen said, we recognize community not as a place to dazzle one another with our talents, but as the place where our poverty is acknowledged and accepted . . . as a true source of new life.

I have a dream that you, too, have a dream.

What is *your* dream? It will come to you, if you don't feel it already. And when it comes, please feel it to your very core, so that when your new friend at college or at your new job asks, "Who are you?," the answer bubbles out of you irrepressibly, like when I watch the inexhaustible Gustavo Dudamel conduct a symphony, jumping to his feet, wild head of floppy black curls flinging back and forth and arms pumping, or when I watch poet-activist Andrea Gibson stand before a microphone, the sheer force of her voice and passion and conviction making her far taller than her petite self. These are people with passion. Yours will express itself in another, different way. Find it. Find it.

The essays in this chapter ask us to consider as fully valid our dreams, our feelings, our loves; to ask ourselves, "What do I feel?," not "Why am I feeling that way?" That "why" question implies we need to validate our feelings—no validation is needed. Feel them. They ask us to feel deeply—that embodied feeling, not just in our heads—to follow the idea that calls us, to have a bold, hot dream and to listen to the bold, hot dreams of others and recognize ourselves in them sometimes.

—*contributed by Kim Joris*

—contributed by Wendee Higa Lee

Follow the idea that calls you

As you start on your own life's passage, follow the idea that makes you wake in the morning without an alarm, that calls you to scribble ideas on napkins and scrap paper and to lose all sense of time, that makes your heart beat faster at every corner with the endless possibilities.

Follow the scent of cookies baking, new places, perfumed air, paint, chalk dust, or newly turned soil that calms your shoulders. Follow the clamor of debate, the clang of pots, the clatter of fingers on a keyboard, the bang of the hammer, or the ringing of bells that is music to your ears.

Follow the caress of another's skin, the rough hew of wood, the jagged edge of glass, or the feel of a fine silk. Follow the colors of paint, the lines of a poem, the elegantly decorated cake, or the bright eyes of another that you see when your own eyes close at night.

—*contributed by Carol A. Sanders*

Feel your feelings

To supplement my financial aid, I work part-time helping a woman organize her home office. She has the cutest two-year-old son named Morgan. The other day Morgan was chomping on bite-size pieces of homemade pizza with thick doughy crust when he bit his tongue. Immediately he started wailing. "I hurt my tongue, Mommy," he cried, looking at her wide-eyed, confused by the pain. She rubbed his back and let him cry, assuring him, "Oh, it hurts, doesn't it? Awww, it probably tastes funny too. Awww . . . bean."

In less than a minute, the tears subsided. "I feel better now." Morgan took a deep breath, wiped his tears, and then popped some pizza into his mouth. Chewing slowly he turned and asked his mom, "Why I was so sad?"

Morgan reminded me how to deal with the unexpected pain that comes with life—and how to help myself and others deal with that pain:

Let them feel their feelings. Let them cry. Or yelp. Or scream. Let them acknowledge where it hurts in their body.

Be there when someone turns to you for support. Be someone who will listen without judging. Hold them without fixing. Affirm their pain then remind them: You're going to be okay.

Let them announce when the pain subsides, then proceed with life as usual.

Ask yourself (and them) the right questions. Instead of "Why me?" or "What did I do wrong?," get curious about what you can learn from it.

—contributed by Ije Ude

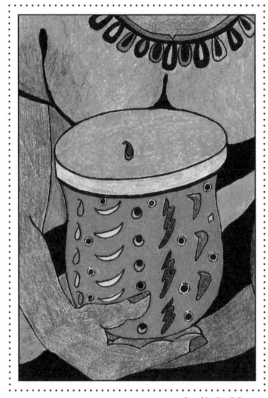

—contributed by Sarah Davis

May your regrets be from loving too much

Do not be afraid to love. Open your heart wide. Throw back the curtains. Let the sun in. Prop the front door open, make a pitcher of lemonade, invite the world! You never know whom you might meet. Don't be afraid to fall in love with ideas, with places, with subjects, with people. You'll fall in and out of love many times, but this is how we figure it out. This is how we learn what we love, this is how we recognize what we want, this is how we know what we need and, maybe just as important, what we do not need. But if we don't immerse ourselves in this crazy life in the first place, we never get the chance.

Sometimes it will seem easier not to throw yourself into the fray. You could get disappointed. You could be rejected. You could get hurt. Better to be the one doing the disappointing, the rejecting, the hurting. That's the easier way, it seems. But my most poignant regrets are of the times I could have rushed headlong into love—into life!—and did not, out of fear.

If you take a chance on love, you might regret it. But maybe we can only hope to end up with the right regrets. Ideas, places, and (especially) people will disappoint you. They will wound you. They will not live up to your standards. But they will also astonish you. They will amaze you. They will bring you more joy than you could imagine. I wish you as much luck and love as possible, with as few regrets as possible. But if they happen (and they probably will), may your regrets be from loving too much instead of not enough.

—*contributed by Gabrielle Kaasa*

—*contributed by Lisa K. Smith*

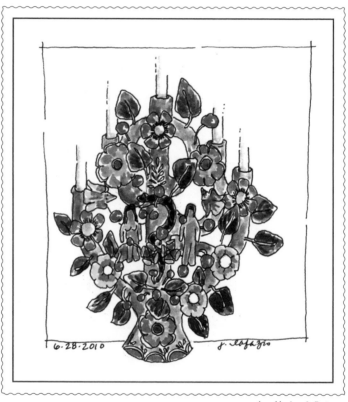

6·28·2010   *J. LaFazio*

—contributed by Jane LaFazio

Coach your heart to be kind

Let your heart be the heart of the matter. Be honest with your heart, be generous, even if it hurts to do so. Coach your heart to be kind, content, peaceful, and to assume the best in others.

Smile. People really don't expect it. If you see a woman with gorgeous eyes, a child who behaves well, someone wearing a cute pair of shoes, tell them. It is delightful to spread joy in this way. And delightful to be the recipient.

There are those in the world who will give you a label. You are not required to accept it. What other people think of you doesn't in any way have to define one single thing about you.

Love is a verb. It is not what you feel, but how you act.

—contributed by Felecia Krech

Take time to just be

In times of transition, please take the time to just be. Sleep in if you'd like, all day if you are able. Sit in your favorite sitting spot. Listen to music, light a candle, eat good chocolate, whatever it is that makes your heart happy as you sit. Color, scrapbook, take photos, read. Cook something that you enjoy to eat, cook something that you've never cooked before. Walk around the block. Do something in nature. Look up at the sky—the sunrise, the clouds, the sunset, the moon, the stars. Listen to the wind. Let the trees, the grass, the air speak to you.

Enjoy quiet time with yourself. Then continue honoring this alone time throughout the rest of your life. You will come to appreciate and treasure all that you find as you allow yourself to just be.

—contributed by Joy Holland

—contributed by Monica K. Dahl

You have what you need to stay afloat

As you embark on this journey, this transition, don't try to
be, just be.

Feel the fear, cry the tears, smile for what is yet to come and
for the memories you've already made.

Let yourself flounder; don't try to have all the answers.

Because you won't.

Explore.

Experiment.

Dream.

Live.

You're on your own time line, you can do things your way.

Be not afraid to go against the grain, to live on your own
terms, to speak out for who you are and what you believe
in.

Take classes just because they sound fun, do things you've
never done and never thought you would.

You are your own lifeboat; you have what you need to stay
afloat.

The waters will be calm, they'll be choppy; some days you'll
row with all your might, even going against the current,
and on others you'll relax and ride the waves.

Create your own reality.

Live the life you've always wanted.

Be your own lifeboat.

—contributed by Sarah Love

—*contributed by Robert C. Ballard*

—*contributed by Lisa Call*

May you . . .

May you live your life fully with wisdom, passion, and humor.

May you base your decisions on knowledge and personal
conviction and not be swayed by popular opinion or
media hype.

May you have the strength to question, then form your own
conclusion.

If you witness an injustice, may you have the courage to act,
speak your mind, and stand up for what you believe in.

May you have compassion for all living beings regardless of
race, gender, or species.

May you laugh loudly and often.

May you always feel loved.

—contributed by Wendy Cook

CHAPTER 3

Make peace with time: *be present*

—*contributed by Ruth M. Davis*

*a*s I prepared to go to my thirtieth high school reunion a few years ago (wait, let me just take a deep breath and realize that I actually wrote those words and they were true), I woke up one Tuesday morning a week and a half before the event, looked in the mirror after my morning shower, and thought to myself one singular thought: "I really should have moisturized more often."

This revelation came just a few weeks after a visit with Emma to the eye doctor where she would try contact lenses for the first time. "I should try contacts again," I said to the doctor, purely to make small talk as she measured the deep, quiet pools of Emma's huge blue eyes. "But the last eye doctor I went to told me I was too old, that my eyes were too dry."

"Oh, that's just not true!" she said. "Why, I have some patients in their seventies who wear contact lenses just fine."

Emma swallowed a laugh. I wondered if the good doctor thought I was Emma's grandmother. That's when the moisturizing thought first occurred to me, I imagine. "Oh," I joked, "I really couldn't do that because at this point, the only thing holding up my sagging eyelids is my glasses frames."

"Oh!" she said. "We can take care of that for you, too!" Turns out, they not only measure your astigmatism but also do wee eye tucks while you wait for your lenses to be ground. Color me shocked. Of course, I was well into my forties before I realized that almost every woman I met above the age of thirty was coloring her hair in some way. Having been raised by a mother who to this very day has never had so much as a manicure or a pedicure, perhaps I missed the self-care and preservation portion of education.

But suddenly here I was staring down my thirtieth high school reunion with something akin to a wild panic. Not so much at the comparisons I thought would inevitably occur *(She looks fabulous, her not so much, wow she hasn't aged well, who are all these old people?)*, but because for the first time I realized at a deeply physical level that I was aging. And would die.

That's a little bit of crazy-making, that realization. I was uncomfortable during that whole reunion as I searched the facial structures of classmates for a clue about who they were, who they now are. And yet with 1970s music blaring, there was little time for even the simplest acknowledgment that by this time in our lives, we had all lived through significant joy and significant pain—those important juxtapositions that create our days. We each had stories of our journey from the then to the now in that room, but very few were told that evening.

A girl/woman I had known since first grade came running over to see me during the reunion, and picked me up in a hug. "You look just like your mother!" she screamed. It might have been the most perfect moment of the evening, it took my breath away so thoroughly.

We live so much in the past, and in the future, and so little in the now, I was thinking to myself. My now would be telling you what and who I love, how much zinnias absolutely thrill me, how scared I am sometimes when I realize I will die and leave my two daughters behind without me. My now would hold you and say, "I adore you for coming to the reunion with

—contributed by Denita L. Purser

me so I wouldn't have to walk in those doors alone." My now would say, "I am the happiest I have ever been and that doesn't mean that I'm not depressed sometimes." My now would say, "I'd like to know you now and I can't remember a lot of the things you're telling me we did in high school anyway."

I recently gave away all the clothes in my closet that I had held on to for fifteen years thinking I would fit back into them. Every single piece of clothing came out of my closet, and the only ones that went back in were ones that I can fit into now—and that I love. The rest went to Goodwill. I woke up the next morning, threw open my closet door, and realized two things: (1) I had made peace with the spectacular now, finally; and (2) I had nothing to wear.

Ram Dass said "Be here now." When we're young and people are constantly telling us to plan for the future and get our résumés in order and major in _____ because there's good money in _____, it's hard to be here now. We feel pressured to be forty with a good retirement fund. But the only thing that matters is the quality of your engagement with the now, the only here there is. If I had known that before I went to my reunion, I would have been happier there, not only with myself, but with dancing to bad loud music and talking to people who for the life of me I couldn't place.

It may be inconceivable to you now that time will pass so quickly, so there's no point in my telling you that. But it will, and one day you will bemoan your own moisturizing habits, and that's how life moves forward. Evolution is messy, after all. Life is incremental, like erosion or like a pattern of growth in the rings of a tree. You choose.

The best days of your life won't be the ones you expect them to be, but they will happen. I remember being in the countryside in Virginia one day with friends having a picnic lunch and eating the best apple I have ever tasted. You won't know which moments will stand out for you later; you can't know. It doesn't matter—live them all anyway. Because right now is always the best moment of your life, and the time will pass anyway.

—*contributed by Jill Osler*

The best days of your life will sneak up on you

At my high school, Class Night was a bigger deal than graduation. On Class Night the principal gave individual seniors awards from each different department; the teachers in that department chose the winners based on grades and participation and general enthusiasm. I'd been involved with music, theater, and the school newspaper for years and thought for sure I'd get at least one award.

I went home empty-handed, devastated.

Sixteen years later I don't remember who won the awards I coveted at Class Night. I do remember the trophy our show choir won the week before graduation. I remember opening night of our spring musical. I remember sitting at my best friend's kitchen table, laughing as we put together the "senior predictions" issue of the school newspaper. I remember sitting on the porch for an entire day that summer, lost in Pamela Dean's *Tam Lin*. I remember seeing *Singing in the Rain* at the Muny, my legs sticking to the seat in the humid summer evening as I sang along under my breath.

Those big milestone days that everyone tells you will be the best days of your life—graduation, wedding, your twenty-first birthday—don't count on them. Don't build them up to be The Only Day That Matters. The best days of your life will sneak up on you. You'll be sitting in your friend's living room after a day of decorating her house for the silliest theme party you could have ever imagined; you'll grin at each other, and you'll realize that you've just experienced one of the Best Days. Those days are amazing gifts, but you can't plan for them. No matter what movies and TV tell you, there is no universal day on which every person in the world will experience true happiness. Right now, graduation or _____ might seem like the day you've been living for, but the fact is, it's the living you've been doing that counts.

—contributed by Jaime Wurth

—contributed by Wendy Cook

Stay Close

When sorrow comes
to those you love
stay close.

When sadness is
more powerful
than words
more powerful
than deeds
your warm hand
your quiet company
your self in a chair
saying nothing
will be a gift.

You may wonder
"What can I do?"
There may be
nothing
you can do.

—contributed by *Carol Sloan*

You may wish
to run.
Do not run.

Hold hands.
Eat soup.
Listen.
Trace a sunbeam
with your fingers
on the table.

Let yourself smile.
Let yourself cry.

When sorrow comes
to those you love
stay close.

When sorrow comes
to you
let others
stay close too.

—contributed by Amy Ludwig VanDerwater

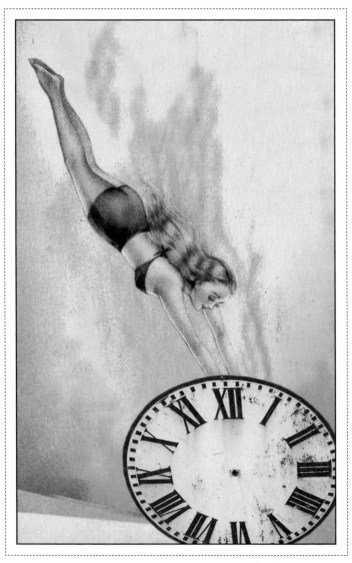

—contributed by Hollis G. Fouts

The time will pass anyway

Many years ago, I was trying to decide whether to go to law school. I had a bachelor's degree in psychology and worked as a legal secretary, the only job I could get. Over the course of a year, I realized I was interested in the law. But if I went to law school, I would have to pay for it myself, which meant I would have to work full-time and go at night. It would take at least another four years.

I decided to apply, and when I actually got accepted I panicked about what to do. So I did what any mature, confident young woman would do.

I called my mother.

I earnestly explained my dilemma: "Mom, I'll be twenty-six years old when I get out of law school!"—which at that point in my life seemed really old.

My mother paused, then very calmly said, "But Susan, you'll be twenty-six whether you're in law school or not."

I went to law school.

When confronted with a challenge that will take a lot of your time, don't focus on how much time it will take. Focus on whether it's how you want to spend your time. Because the time will pass anyway.

—*contributed by Susan R. Meisinger*

Age is the secret

While we often fear aging, AGE is the secret to a happy life:

> A = Assist others
> G = Gratitude
> E = Exercise

Assist others. So often we go through life on cruise control. Stop and conscientiously look for ways to help out others. It may be holding a door for someone, asking a new student to sit next to you during lunch, or helping out with an organization about which you feel passionate. Reaching out to others not only helps them, but also helps you.

Gratitude. We all know that there are ups and downs in life. Experiencing and expressing gratitude helps you to feel happier, have better relationships, be more productive, and enjoy a healthier life. Every day write out at least three positive things that happen to you and things that you are proud of doing.

Exercise. Exercise is vital for every body and mind. Not only does exercise do wonders for us physically (helps cholesterol, prevents arteriolosclerosis, helps us sleep), but it's also great for our psychological health (reduces stress and depression, boosts happiness, improves self-confidence, enhances creativity). Make exercise a part of your life now and forever.

AGE with grace.

—contributed by Elizabeth Lombardo

—contributed by Kathryn Ruth Schuth

—contributed by Patti Bourne

Right now is always the best moment of your life

My kids sometimes ask, "Mommy, what was your favorite age?" I answer truthfully, "The age I am."

Right now is always the best moment of your life.

Learn from and laugh about the past, build and dream for the future, but live now. Be fully in the present. Extract every bit of nowness surrounding you and absorb it into your cells. With every experience, every thought, and every feeling, more of who you are emerges.

You are doing something, thinking something, feeling something right now—good, bad, cheesy, brilliant, joyful, painful, dull, thrilling, or a million other possibilities. And it is *wonderful.* You will never have a moment exactly like this one again. That's wonderful, too.

Being in the now makes it easier to handle anything, regret nothing, and love life and everyone and everything in it in all their wonderful, endearing imperfection. Nothing is over-whelming, insurmountable, or unforgivable when it is consid-ered in moment-size parcels. Conversely, the tsunami of joy that can surge through your soul in a single moment defies rea-son. It's a beautifully imbalanced equation.

Right now is always the best moment of your life.

—*contributed by Michelle Drabik*

Be interested in their story

When you meet new people, treat them as if you already know and love them. So when you talk to someone or invite that person into a circle (be on the lookout for those outside the circle—they need friends, too), or when you approach someone else standing by themselves, talk to them and be friendly as if you know them already.

Be inquisitive, make eye contact; be interested in their story.

—contributed by Gloria Wooldridge

—*contributed by Margaret Williams*

CHAPTER 4

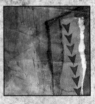

Let go of certainty: *be unsure*

—*contributed by Leah Piken Kolidas*

I grew up in a small southern town where nobody knew the street names, but just gave directions by landmarks and events: Turn left where the Biltmore Dairy building burned down, go straight past the pool hall where Uncle Guy "Frog" Ramsey got shot in the face, turn right at Mull's Feed and Seed (where evidently nothing of note happened other than the rambunctious selling of feed and seed).

Life was predictable and orderly. I had to vacuum and dust on Saturday mornings while my brother got to mow the grass simply because he was male, but I've worked through all my post-existential phenomenological feminist anger about that. Thursday night was the miracle of Swanson's frozen Chicken Pot Pies, Friday night was hushpuppies and other fried objects (with that tiny-chopped-runny coleslaw I love) from the Fish Camp near the Putt-Putt, Saturday was steak-and-potatoes and shoe-polishing night. Gilligan, Lucy, Bobby Sherman, and Lawrence Welk were old friends who dropped by daily or at the very least, weekly. Like Swiss trains running inevitably on a Southern Baptist schedule, we were at Calvary Baptist every Sunday, a day during which no card- or game-playing could occur, including Go Fish and especially that evil icon of capitalist society and materialistic greed, Monopoly.

When I was sixteen I left orderliness and entered into a vast unknown by getting on an airplane for the very first time, by myself, my parents watching and no doubt crying from a window at the Charlotte Douglas International Airport. I boarded a flight that would deposit me in a country that until just a month earlier I had never even heard of, some 12,000 miles away from home. Sri Lanka was my destination, a tiny island country that used to be known as Ceylon, off the tip of India.

I would live there with a Sinhalese family in a small village, study with Buddhist monks, eat rhombutans straight off the tree, navigate bathrooms without toilet paper or toilet seats, be an apprentice in a batik factory, attend Museus Buddhist Girls' College, and laugh with a "sister" in that family, a girl so unlike me and so like me all at the same time.

I learned at that young age to give up certainty and to embrace confusion. There was little around me there that looked familiar. I was in a different world from the moment I stepped onto that Air India jet in New York City that took me first to India, and then to Colombo, Sri Lanka. Flight attendants dressed in beautiful saris brought me unknown foods like rice and curry IN THE AIR. I had never flown before, so each moment was a revelation, the sunrises and sunsets that set the tiny airplane windows on fire so numerous I hardly knew when one day began and another ended.

Because lightning had hit our plane in New York City before departure, we were delayed leaving, missing our connection in Madras for Colombo. That delay threw off the entire schedule for language training in Sri Lanka and so we exchange students landed with the ability to say hello in Sinhalese and not much else. A family arrived at the airport, picked me up, and the uncertain adventure began.

We all come into the world not knowing, and we try to know immediately. We explore, question, try things out as toddlers. And then our capacity for not knowing calcifies as we age. School, at least in our Western culture, is predicated on knowing. Not knowing is not rewarded, but punished. We learn quickly that to know is to win, and so being unsure is a sign of weakness, not to be tolerated.

Peter Block has written that the answer to "how" is "yes." We are addicted to how, a question that insinuates that the answer is somewhere out there, that there is a "best practice" or a way that someone else can give us. A bajillion-dollar self-help industry is built on this assumption—that we are broken if we don't know, and an "expert" can tell us the answer. This falsehood has pathologized not knowing. We need to reclaim that state of being unsure, that surge of energy that hits us mid-chest when we realize we can't read the street signs and don't have the first clue which bathroom is for men, and which for women. Those places of just-enough anxiety propel us into life.

Reclaiming un-knowing is a focus of these essays. Reveling in failure, being open to getting lost, and living in a world of questions, not answers—these are vital. There is no place for boredom in a world full of newness.

—contributed by Stacey Beth Shulman

Be a failed artist

I loved being an artist. Breathed it. It's what I was. But I was always terrified of becoming a *failed* artist. Couldn't stand the idea of going broke doing it. I heard the warnings: No money in it. No way to make a living. I loved it so much I was scared to death to even try to be it.

So I gave it up. Never gave myself a chance to fail at it. Tried to be something more conventional, something "with a future" . . . and searched twenty years looking for what else I was supposed to be.

I never did find that out. But I did find a lot of ways to be a kind-of, almost-visible, incognito artist impersonating something else.

And all that other stuff still happened to me.

How much more fun life can offer if we allow ourselves to be instead of trying to be something. In thirty-seven days or thirty-five years you'll be what you are—the difference is how much you listen to your own voice. You can't go too broke remembering that.

—*contributed by Jeremy Reynolds*

Take the long look

Now that you're entering a world in which your time and attention will be divided into a million quick glances a day just to make sure you're not missing anything, I want to remind you to *take the long look as often as you can*. The challenge is to find the beauty in the most ordinary things—not just the extraordinary ones. If you do this, your life will be so full of beauty and you will feel like the richest person on the planet.

Taking the long look won't fix anything that's already broken, and it won't make your life easier, but it will give you a perspective on life that will allow you to face adversity with grace, receive blessings with gratitude, and recognize what life really has to offer you. Sift through all the hours in a day to find the glimmer, the shiny minute, the pure moment, the poetry.

—*contributed by Feithline Stuart*

—contributed by Dian K. McCray

—*contributed by Mahima Shrestha*

Be wary of advice

Was it your idea to even want all this advice? This is what I'm wondering. I have no idea what life will bring you or what you'll choose.

Use a compass.

Go in directions that are familiar.

For instance, you know that feeling you get when you are driving up to see your horse and you're getting close to the stable? Let that be your north.

You know that feeling you get when you are laughing so hard that you might have to change your underwear? Let that be your south.

You know that feeling you get when you're riding your horse and jumping and sensing all that power and all that wind on your face? Let that be your east.

You know that feeling you get when someone you love texts or calls or shows up by surprise? Let that be your west.

In other words, you have a whole lifetime of knowing what's good and true, what delights you and frightens you and makes you fall in like and in love.

Trust your self. Listen in.

I think you already know how to do this. I'm reminding you to keep doing it. My advice? Be wary of advice.

—contributed by Jodi Cohen

Ask yourself this question often

Ask yourself this question often: "What do I see when I see people?"

Like all good questions, this will slow you down. And slowing down when it comes to judging others will make you gentle and keep you kind.

Because the first thing we see when we meet others is their mask. But if you pause and think a bit, you'll see someone like you. Someone's child. Someone who is uncertain. Someone looking for a star to guide them.

It's always easier to be kind when you know "they" are struggling just like you.

—contributed by Mike Wagner

—contributed by *Jennifer L. Cohen Incorvaia*

Get lost

In today's world, no one gets lost anymore. We pull up a GPS on our cell phones, type in our destination, and get step-by-step directions to where we want to go. Many of us also have a mental map, a personal GPS as it were, telling us where we want to go in our life. It's great to have an idea of where you want to go and how to get there, but you can gain even more when you veer off your map. You join a friend in a volunteer activity and meet someone there who changes your life. Perhaps you go to a lecture or concert that sounds boring and it ignites a passion that leads you in a direction you would otherwise never have traveled. You take up a hobby and it becomes central to your life. Something unexpected—a failure perhaps—pushes you off your map and becomes the catalyst that leads you to a more exciting, challenging life path.

If you never jump off the path, you lose the adventure that can come when you lose your way. You miss the joy of finding a new path. It's great to have a map. I wouldn't visit a new city without one. But in life the best possibilities are often those that come when you wander. You have the opportunity to get lost, to turn back, or to turn in a whole new direction. You can explore, try new things, and take chances. You can stop and see something new. It's nice to have an idea of where you will go or what you will do with your life, but try not to let your ideas become unalterable routes.

May your journeys lead you down new paths. May you find adventure, take risks, and explore as you continue down the road of your life.

—contributed by Rabbi Julie Wolkoff

—contributed by Kathryn Antyr

CHAPTER 5

Learn something every day: *be curious*

—contributed by Lie Fhung

*Y*ears after college my beloved physics professor, Sheri-dan Simon, told me that the bane of his existence was delivering a simply beautiful lecture on the physics of black holes or quantum mechanics, then opening the floor to questions knowing he had done some of his best work, only to have the student in the second row raise his hand to ask: "Will this be on the test?"

Voltaire has said, "Judge a man by his questions rather than by his answers." Why are we learning anything in life? To sati-ate our own curiosity or because it will be on the test? This is a vital distinction—not only for students, but also for busi-ness executives and parents and all the rest of us. The pursuit of knowing—and, more important, of not knowing—this is curiosity. And curiosity keeps us alive, pure and simple.

Honest inquiry. Honest inquiry is the pursuit of great, fan-tastic, compelling questions posed for one reason: to explore. Not to pass the test, but to explore. What a planet we live on! Where do rivers go? Is there a cloud factory? How do birds know when to go, and when to come back? Why is Justin Bieber famous? From where does racism come?

How can we remain curious? As Bernard Baruch said, "Millions saw the apple fall, but Newton asked why." How can we recapture the holy curiosity of our childhood in which "why" was our way of being in the world? Here are a few ways:

Play backup. A few years ago I was asked to give a keynote talk at a conference in Melbourne, Australia. A brilliant man named Charles Hampden-Turner (who eventually became my intellectual mentor and who, at the time, had written something like twenty books) was the opening speaker of the conference; I was the closing speaker. The very thought of meeting him and being near him—much less giving a speech in front of him—made me very nervous. During the conference, in addition to my keynote, I was also to give a workshop. Who should show up but Charles Hampden-Turner, to listen and to learn. What on earth could I possibly say that would be of interest to this amazing intellect? It didn't matter. What mattered was that he came and he listened and he laughed and participated. He played backup, not leading man. I have watched him do it repeatedly since then. This is the mark of curiosity, the showing up, the willingness, the spongelike quality even in someone who has so much to teach others.

Name your intention. I co-facilitated a training session once that was, admittedly, not the best training design in which I had participated; mostly I wanted to live through the three days and go have a beer or sob. But there I was, making the best of it, and with a room full of learners save three people who decided their mission was to make me even more painfully aware of the flaws in the design, and—most important—how much better they could do it than me. Their mission was not curiosity, but ridicule. Theirs was not a mind-set of learning. They would do nothing in those three days except close down learning, for themselves and for others. Naming your intention is vital: Are you learning to pass the test, to show off or show down, to get a promotion? Or to learn?

Never be bored. Really? You're bored? Because you've already read every book, talked to every person in your universe about what they love to think about, and you know exactly how ice crystals form and how planes stay up in the sky? Wow. Albert Einstein tells us, "The important thing is not to stop questioning. Curiosity has its own reason for existing . . . Never lose a holy curiosity." What is your reason for boredom? That the world isn't entertaining enough for you? Or that it has not focused its considerable appeal on you, specifically and totally you? Boredom is for the selfish. Don't go there.

Focus on ideas. "Be less curious about people and more curious about ideas," advised Marie Curie. What makes up the bulk of your dinnertime conversation: people, events, or ideas? Move in the direction of ideas.

Seek disequilibrium. Learning involves discomfort. More often than not, it involves the discomfort of not knowing. We're trained to know. As Einstein said, it's a miracle curiosity survives formal education, so deeply ingrained is the goal to have the right answer. But learning—real learning—involves not knowing. As Marie Curie has also said (smart woman!), "Dissymmetry causes phenomena." Things don't happen until they are thrown off balance. How can you throw yourself off balance? Alter your daily routine: When you go to the movies, are you an aisle-seat-in-the-back sitter? Sit middle front to alter your perspective. Enroll in a class about which you know nothing, exactly nothing, not the one that will be a breeze. Read magazines you'd never pick up. Seek opportunities for disequilibrium rather than running from them.

Listen to children. Never interrupt a child. Never lose patience with their endless series of questions. Find opportunities to hear a child's perspective on anything, everything. Here are a few examples of the questions Tess asks us daily: "If the world was disinvented, where would we be?" and "What was the first word ever spoken?" Children teach us, if we don't ignore them or shut them down because we falsely believe we know better.

Be a fearless experimenter. Our seven-year-old is a fearless tiny maniac in the kitchen. She started by making vegetable soup, cutting up broccoli and carrots and adding them to broth. And then she started experimenting. Orange juice base, into which she put grapes, red pepper, tomato, thyme, carrots, lemon juice, watermelon, and more. I'm not sure why, but the very idea of it made me a bit pukey, so I feared the inevitable "TRY IT! IT'S GREAT! TRY IT!" But try it I did, and many others of her experiments, and it was . . . delicious! I see *Top Chef* in Tess's future, for sure. Why? Because she doesn't have categories of fruit versus vegetable in her head—yet. She flings her produce together, as should we all.

Ask many questions. Simply ask "why" ten times a day. Stop long enough to listen to the answer, or seek the answer yourself.

Make elaborate gestures. Life needs to include more elaborate gestures pointed in the direction of other people. Because it means we are paying attention, that we are curious about them. I recently spent an entire day traveling by car and plane and plane and car from my home in Asheville, North Carolina, to Hastings, Nebraska. When I checked into my hotel room, a big gift bag awaited me that included, among many other fantastic things, all the makings for in-room DIY s'mores (candle, marshmallows, Hershey's, graham crackers, metal on which to hold the marshmallows) and a copy of a book by poet Ted Kooser, signed especially for me because I love his poetry. One way into curiosity is to show up for someone today. Maybe that means a well-chosen gift bag that shows you're in tune with someone. Maybe it just means picking up the phone, leaving some daffodils on someone's porch, telling someone a story that will encourage her, accepting the invitation to take a walk together, writing a letter to someone you haven't connected with in a while, sending some encouragement through the airwaves to a friend who seems down or overwhelmed, helping a friend pack and move, choosing acceptance over blame, or including an extra stop in your next trip. Show up for others today. It is an expression of curiosity about them.

Be a generous learner. My business partner, David Robinson, and I often fling learners into completely unknown territory in which there is no right answer, only the experience they are having at that moment. Learning stops for those who turn with a quizzical look to ask, "Am I doing this right?" "You are doing it right because you are doing it that way," we often say. Assume there is no right, only the experience you are having at the moment. Granted, your professor may have a different "right," but genuine inquiry into the experience you are having is worth more IQ points than recapitulating what someone else deems is right. There is no way to learn while judging. I can either learn, or I can judge myself (or others) for what I don't know, but I can't do both those things at the same time. Choose learning. Much less painful.

It's all on the test, sugar. Learn—and unlearn and relearn—accordingly.

> *There is a certain serendipity to living life as if it were all going to be on the exam—juicing life like a morning orange. These essays celebrate learning, exploration, failing. They challenge us to take many trips, see the beauty in everything around us, to celebrate failure, to create new measures of success. The way into ourselves is to learn something every day.*

—contributed by Hollis G. Fouts

—contributed by Rebecca E. Parsons

Find the beauty

Find the beauty.
It is everywhere and in nearly everything.
It is in truth and in places least expected.
It is right in front of us where we sometimes cannot see.
Find the beauty.
It is always worth living for.

—*contributed by R. L. Delight*

Cut yourself some slack

Economies change, definitions change, people come and go—you need to create a balance within yourself. Pace yourself. You may find yourself in a free fall of sorts, and having things you can rely on when all the other variables change will help you find and keep your center.

Sports, reading, writing, gardening, cooking, meditation, and creating art are all things you can practice throughout a lifetime. Find good true friends to share them with. Develop your personal strengths and passions, then cultivate them continuously. Know when you need to be alone and carve out some time for a walk, a ride, time in the woods or by a lake. Take your worries there and let them go.

Get to know people and take them for their word; don't interpret people to meet your vision of who you want them to be. It won't work. Listen to them and really hear what they are saying. If it doesn't align with what you want in your life, consider looking in a different direction. This means you need to know what you want. Bending is one thing, breaking quite another. Don't let others break you.

If there is enticement that draws you to a person, place, or job that you have doubts about, be honest with yourself and your expectations about what is being offered. It may be money, status, visibility, excitement—just be honest about what it is that draws you. Know that there may be things for you to learn there. But remember that people do not change, you cannot make them appreciate your efforts, gifts, or love. Be selective of who you invite into your life. Don't be weary of the world but do listen honestly to it. Most of all just live your life, be there, show up, and cut yourself a lot of slack.

—contributed by Betsy L. Edwards

—contributed by Gwyn Michael

—contributed by Liz Kettle

Question the questions

Questions are more important than answers. Rushing in to find stuff out meant I lost a lot of questions on the way in.

I've learned it's better to be open than closed, and better to be unsure than sure . . . that it's better to see a horizon as a place to enjoy rather than as an imaginary limit.

Questioning the answers is great, but questioning the questions is more powerful. Questions are a part of curiosity, and curiosity is the engine of the imagination. Like these questions, from my children over the years, most of which I had never heard or thought of before: "Why doesn't rain fall up?" "Why are stars so messy?" "Why do we have only one sun and how come it moves so slowly?" "Do you have to stay in the lines in a coloring book?" Elementary questions, perhaps, but they demand elegant answers.

Getting to an answer can shave the edges off the question; and it is in those "shaved-off" parts—those rough edges, the stuff that rubs up against your comfort zones—that you'll find ways to learn, to be creative, to be imaginative.

—*contributed by John Ptak*

Take every trip you can

Seek and create community. Always. And never forget that you play a key role in the formation of any type of community that you join. When you are sitting around waiting for an invitation to do amazing things and have grand adventures, and the calls and texts don't come, this is your cue that you need to be the one sending the texts and making the calls. It's your turn to gather.

We all have our poverties. Learn to understand this about every single person you meet, and to recognize your own.

Don't wait for permission. You are your own permission.

Sometimes, when you run out of clean underwear, it's a better tactic to go buy some than to do laundry.

Take every trip you can.

And this is the most important thing of all: Play. In all that you do: Play.

That's all. Trust yourself. Be worthy of your trust. And play with all your heart, with all the tools life has given you.

And write your mother.

—contributed by Kathryn Ruth Schuth

—contributed by Julie Galante

—*contributed by Patricia L. Watson*

Nothing is wasted

Because you are a lover and an artist, you will have occasion (many, actually) to open your chest, pull out a ruby, offer it to The World (or someone in The World) . . . and it will be received with as much enthusiasm as a piece of gum.

Chewed, slathered upon, and spat.
Out.

This happens to ruby-hearted people who are responsible for bringing through every shade of red in the spectrum, from the gentlest pink to the baddest-assed bordeaux. This is no small role to play—carrying around rubies in your heart—and offering the spectrum of red, the tastes of strawberries and mesquite, the squealing sounds of pain and delight, the heat of hugs and blazes.We, heart-bearers of red rubies, love and create like no one's business because, for us, it ain't business. It's beingness.

And on those days when your beingness feels
chewed, slathered upon, and spat.
Out.
KNOW—know—know that nothing is wasted.

Everything is useful for the deepening of your pigment the deliciousizing of your flavor, the longevity of your flames. It's all good. Eventually. Assuredly. Good. All of it.

—contributed by Erika Harris

Live in the library

Live in the library. Bring a pillow if they'll let you. Find a cozy carrel and move in. Of course, you've used a library before, but I mean really live in it. Don't settle for merely being well-read, but let yourself become deep read, crazy deep read, and uniquely read.

Let serendipity lead you to sections of the stacks you wouldn't normally wander. Social histories of everything. Reference books of everything. Newspapers from little towns around your state with unusual news and announcements. Maps, photographs, government documents. And then there's Special Collections. These are all rich treasures waiting to be unearthed. Let your curiosity get the better of you, even if you have a test the next day. Especially if you have a test the next day.

Forget the catalog. Just explore, floor by floor, section by section. Make friends with the librarians. Live there. Until they make you leave. And then come back again as soon as you can.

—contributed by Celeste Tibbets

—contributed by Eric M. Scott

—contributed by *Mary Campbell*

Learn how to be still

Youth is a restless time with so many vistas that it's hard to focus and pick a direction. Growing older has taught me that it's not any different later in life. I wish I had learned earlier how to be still and wait for a direction to come to me. Stillness has a purpose, and we have to be still before we can grow.

I hope you can learn to be still. To sit with nothing to accomplish but to notice what's around you and what's within you. And trust that what bubbles up is authentic and beautiful and just right.

—contributed by Brandie Sellers

Most important, shine

Don't lose sight of who you are, don't conform, and don't listen to anyone who says "it" can't be done. Stand tall. Be proud of who you are and where you came from. Mostly who you are.

Life doesn't happen to you, you happen to it. Don't lean back in your chair—jump up, take action, lean into it. Choose a career path that you feel like walking on. In bare feet. For a lot of miles.

Listen to the voices in your head, listen to the songs in your heart. They will be your best friends throughout your life.

It's a good idea to have a plan, but it's also a good idea to make room for the unexpected. The possibilities are endless. The time to accomplish them is not. Choose accordingly.

Life is full of mysteries. You won't solve most of them. Accept this, and move on. What makes us all so special is exactly what makes us all the same.

This is the most wonderful, carefree time of your life. You won't believe it until it is over and you are past it. But try. Open your eyes, every day, to the mundane moments. This is what life is made of. Learn to enjoy them, now. Cleaning your room or your mind every so often is not a sacrifice, or a chore; it is a way to make room for your potential.

Most important, shine.

—contributed by Kelly J. Letky

—contributed by *Grace Bower*

Know yourself better than you know anyone else

As you go through life, it's the little moments you'll remember. The ones embedded in the grand events or the ones that hit your heart just right so that it tings. Or those moments when everything changes in your life, and you know it. Start noticing those moments now, and if it moves you, keep a log. These memories are the ones that will carry you home to that place deep inside you and remind you that you were truly here.

Be open and brave in your learning. Ask for what you need so you feel inspired and excited with your assignments, rather than simply giving teachers what they ask for. I promise, you will delight some of your professors or employers.

Realize you will fail sometimes, and that some of your failures may be big. Remember, the important thing is not that you fall, but how fast you get up.

Respect everything, its right to exist. It all matters to someone or something, somehow, somewhere. Respect it all, whether something has significance for yourself or not. For that is where the conversation begins.

Know yourself better than you know anyone else. What moves your heart to tears or joy. What thrills every cell in your being so you cease to exist and merge with it. What stimulates you to drive past any challenge in its pursuit. Where your Bliss resides. Where your boundaries are set, the things you absolutely will not do, places you will not go, no matter what. Know your greatest fear. And what is your abiding question in this life, the one your Soul asks the Universe with everything you do.

Discover the Gift you have to give to the world. We all have one. Embrace the charge to use it, whatever that looks like.

And finally, be open to change. Nothing's constant in our human existence except change. With mindfulness, be its steward.

—contributed by Heloise Jones

—contributed by Lori Gillen

—*contributed by Laura Stinson*

Then do the next thing

You know what's right for you, even though sometimes you won't do it. You'll learn from it all. Not one second of life is wasted; it is all learning, living, loving. There is grace in all of it. There is no need for shame, guilt, or seeking fulfillment or saving from outside of you. You have it all.

You've been rewarded for hard work and equally rewarded when you didn't look like you were working hard enough. Life is the reward. It is enough. Forming a six-pack or a pot belly, those are just different types of work, different steps on the path, with different scenery. All steps are leading to the same place, gradually. You are more than the grade points, the disappointments, the scholarships, the sinking ships. You were be-ing you when your grades sucked and no one cared if they saw you at the dance, the same you that is popular and doing well in school, the same you that lost the game, won the game, the same you that felt under the weather, felt on top of the world. You are always be-ing in unconditional love and you are not alone.

When it becomes a challenge to know that, you can take a breath and be thankful for that breath. Then do the next thing and be grateful for that next thing.

—*contributed by Thomai Hatsios*

"Just remember
to change your oil."
—*Nina McIntosh*

CHAPTER 6

Open up your hand: *be free*

—contributed by Rina Yuriko Francisco

I travel almost every week to give keynote speeches, workshops, retreats, or to facilitate difficult meetings for clients. Delta Platinum status is a blessing—and a curse. What I've learned about travel in my circumnavigations of the globe to over sixty countries above the clouds is also what I've learned about traveling through life:

Travel light. Put every single thing you need for your trip on your bed. Now put half of it away and pack the other half for your trip. Seriously. While you might have a moment's pang of regret that you didn't bring that hand-knit cardigan made for you by an elder in Nova Scotia from the hair of yaks, the regret won't last and you'll get by just fine with the much less bulky shawl you did bring. The same goes for closets, bookcases, the things you hide under your bed or in your crazy basement thinking you might need them one day. *Make do with less.*

Never check luggage. Being agile is important. When things go wrong (the inbound plane is stuck in the Cape Verde Islands because the wing fell off, for example—or your dream job isn't so dreamy), you need to be able to take your own luggage and do a work-around. This can never happen if you've left your luggage in someone else's care, if you've abdicated your responsibility for your belongings to others, a tiny tag the only thing between it and oblivion. *Keep it with you.* (Which means you really must go back to lesson number one and take it seriously.)

Bring your own water bottle. I was amused by the snarky tweets from a recent conference about the lack of power strips available in the room for laptop users to plug into. You need a power strip? You always need one at conferences or in airports where people circle columns with plugs like carrion circling roadkill? Bring it yourself and stop complaining that someone isn't providing for you. Need a snack on the plane? Bring one yourself, or would you rather complain about the lack of food service like that is still news? Save that energy for studying the safety instructions. Stay fully hydrated. Bring your own water bottle, a tiny Sigg bottle with peace signs on it that you can take empty through TSA and fill up at a water fountain once you've re-dressed after the pat-down. *Equip yourself for your own needs.*

Don't expect upgrades. I love upgrades. Love, love, love them. A little breathing space makes my day happier. I used to peruse the Delta site twenty-four hours before every flight like a crack addict looking for a fix, hoping to see upgrade granted. But when I expect them and bank my whole happiness on getting them or not, I fall hard when the first-class cabin fills up and I'm relegated to my tiny perch in what my young child called the "third-class cabin." *Just enjoy the ride!*

Be able to carry your own bags. This has long been my edict. After traveling for years with bags that were too heavy,

I have pared down to something I can pick up. This was for a long time my happy Ogio backpack, but in recent months I've moved to a roll-aboard Ogio Layover bag to save my back. *Be able to pull your own weight.* (Asking for help when you need it is also important, I know.)

Don't rush the line. I don't think I've ever been as mortified as I was while traveling as with a colleague who pushed people aside to make his way to the front of a line to board: "I HAVE A FIRST-CLASS SEAT!" he announced. Then, "PATTI, GET UP HERE WITH ME." Um, no. I'll wait back here with the human beings. *Don't be rude.*

Help others. Young parents with babies on planes are the bane of every business traveler. I know this, having looked at it from both sides now. That young mother or father with the baby or rambunctious toddler is doing the best she or he can. Let's make that assumption, shall we, and extend some empathy and help. Children are tiny miracles, they are. YOU WERE ONE ONCE. A two-hour flight with Emma during which she screamed—and I mean SCREAMED UP A LUNG—during almost the entire flight taught me this. A kind older woman walking up and down the aisle with her for me was the only thing that soothed her. *Help, don't complain.*

Take a book and a sweater. There are a few things I always— always—have with me. One is a book, and one is a sweater (or my interpretation of "sweater," which is "shawl"). You will always have to wait and you will always get chilly. I used to bring several books on a trip in case I got bored with one. I stopped doing that. Now I bring one book, and its sole presence allows for greater focus and determination—I make it through the parts that feel slow to the meaning beneath. It has been a remarkable change, that one thing. Don't prepare for every eventuality—that will burden you. (You do not want to know what all was in the huge bag of survival gear I carried with me right after 9/11, no, you do not.) Go back to the first entry. You'll only need half of what you think is urgently necessary. *Be prepared* for *surprise, not* against *it.*

Call the airline directly. When the inevitable happens—delay, canceled flight—call the airline directly instead of waiting in line to talk to the gate agent. The non-travel equivalent of this is to take care of it yourself, call the person who is disagreeing with you or obstructing you, don't allow someone else to do it for you. Ask for creative solutions. *Go directly to the source.*

Be consistent. I used to have to do my own full-body search when it came time to board the plane: Where is that boarding pass? Now I know. I always carry it in exactly the same place. Always. I reach there automatically now, knowing it will be there. The panic of days past (at least on that issue), gone. Especially because 99 percent of the time I travel wearing my beloved ScotteVest travel vest on which there are hidden pockets, each with its designated contents: Left front vest pocket is phone, right front vest pocket is camera, inner left front pocket is boarding passes, and so forth. It is gloriously compulsive and removes one source of stress from my travel days. Plus, when

I go through security, I just take the whole vest off and, *voilà*, I know I won't make the metal detector sing. *Keep track of your essentials.*

Make people smile. *This is as true of life as it is of travel.* I use Twitter when I travel, mainly to report on my success—or lack of success—in making people smile or laugh, particularly in the worst of circumstances. When you put your focus on the other (my intention is to make you smile or laugh rather than boil in the stew of my own unhappiness at the fact that this flight was just canceled), great things can happen. Maybe you start smiling, too, and then happiness breaks out all over. Don't let your sleepiness, panic, anxiety, horror, or fury get in the way of a good belly laugh. *Laughing can be the best medicine.*

Talk to your seatmates. I know. I know. This is why you love your iPod. Trust me, I have those days, too. But take out your earplugs for a while. Listen to their story, tell them part of yours. I've met some of my closest friends on planes. You may, too. *Be open to other people's stories.*

Thank people. Find people every day to thank. FIND THEM. THEY ARE THERE. Say thank you to the gate agents as they scan your boarding pass. Say thank you to the flight attendant who does the safety demonstration. Tell someone you love their sweater. Admire the baby in 10B. A crew member or hotel staff person does a spectacular job? Get their name. Tell their supervisor. Always. Focusing on what people do right is powerful. Too often we only focus on what goes wrong. I write a thank-you note every morning. It shapes a life of gratitude. *Show your gratitude.*

Stay connected to your human survival units. Call home. It's too easy to get swept up into the fray of the travel. Reach out to the people you've left behind. A quick good morning, a text message to a teenager, a photo to a toddler. Send a sign of your movement through the world to those who matter most. *Check in with those you love.*

Life is a trip, a journey, a trek. How free are you to move through your life? These last few essays are about letting go, being free, traveling through life with wild, fantastic abandon—and living forward. It is hard to do that if you are grasping onto heavy bags, strict rules, rigid beliefs and dreams. Let go a little. Your life is within your hands.

—contributed by Elizabeth Beck

—contributed by Linda Clearwater

It is for you to decide

In a small village there lived a famous rabbi known for having the right answers to all the questions in the world. Many people journeyed to the village to get his all-knowing advice.

Not far from the rabbi's house lived a young guy named Yakov, a smart man who could also be quite rude. Yakov was anxious to find a question the rabbi couldn't answer and finally thought he had come up with such a question: "I'll go to the rabbi holding a butterfly in my hand and ask him what I have in my fist. The rabbi will surely know the answer, but then ask him if the butterfly is dead or alive. If he says it is alive, I'll smash it . . . and if he says it is dead, I'll open my fingers, let it fly and prove him wrong."

The next day, Yakov went to the rabbi and asked him, "Honorable Rabbi, can you tell me what I have in my closed hand?" The rabbi thought for a moment and answered: "Well, I believe you are holding a butterfly."

"That's true, Rabbi, but can you tell me whether it is dead or alive?" asked Yakov with a victorious smile on his face. The rabbi looked at him and then smiled back: "That, my son, is for you to decide. It is within your hands."

It is within your hands. It is for you to decide what kind of life will you have. May you have the wisdom to choose well, the courage to follow those choices, and the ability to love and be loved.

—contributed by Eliav Zakay

Live your life forwards

One day soon you will find yourself needing to make a "big" decision—not about where to go for dinner or what cocktail to order, but a decision that will have consequences. You may have to make many of these during your life. You'll want to make the right or the very best decision, yet how is it possible to know in advance what that is? You may find yourself having a conversation, with yourself most probably, maybe with others, about the "what ifs." What if . . . this happens? What if . . . that happens?

My advice to you is to let go of the "what ifs"—to follow what feels good, to make a decision and move on from that. Who knows where it will take you? No-regrets decision making. Only by looking back when you are much older will you be able to recognize those sliding door moments—those decisions that took you down a path that led you somewhere—or to someone—magical. The trick is to step through doors, not hesitating so long that the door shuts, leaving you wondering what might have been. What if . . . ?

The Danish philosopher Kierkegaard said, "You can only understand life backwards, but we must live it forwards." Live your life forwards.

—contributed by Viv McWaters

—*contributed by Louise Gale*

Give the kind of love you have

One thing I wish I would have known earlier in my life is this . . . the love you take into your heart as you live your days is going to come from many different people. You hear often in stories and songs and movies about the ONE person whose love will be everything to you, who will be everything you ever needed. What you will find, however, is that people give what they have. We are wired differently, and we will give our love differently. You will find people whose love feeds your mind, and people whose love feeds your sense of humor, and people whose love you can count on at 2:00 a.m. on a random Tuesday. When you let all of those different kinds of love into your spirit, it will smooth out the rough spots, filling in the tiny spaces left behind from moments of pain and misunderstanding. One person may not fill the role of providing every kind of love you need, and that is what makes life interesting. When you let different people play the parts they are best at playing, it allows them to simply be who they are when they are with you. And when you can give the kind of love you have to the world, you can simply be who you are, giving what you have to give.

People sometimes seem to let us down simply because they don't seem to give us what we need. Try to remember that they are giving what they know, what they've been shown, and what they have. Many of us are carrying much more than we need, and sometimes all that we carry can keep us from seeing all that we are. You can lighten the load for people each time you offer acceptance of their stories, acknowledgment of their songs, and awareness of what makes them unique.

Hold on to the love people have to give, and let go of anything else they've handed you to carry. And keep your own carry-on bag as light as you can, so you can see who you are, where you're going, and what you are leaving behind for the ones you love.

—contributed by Tamara Bailie

—contributed by Kate McGovern

—contributed by *Cathy Kirwan*

All of this takes time

When you leave a community—going off to college, taking a new job, resettling in a different place—what you can and cannot take with you will always be a surprise. It's not only what you can pack in your suitcase, or what you carry, but the feelings, the smells, the space.

When you land in your new community, you will have to create, build, shape, and reestablish that sense of your own belonging—your very own community. It sometimes takes a long time to get it all feeling just right—finding the friends that you can just pick up and go with, finding the perfect spot to curl up and get cozy, exploring and finding the perfect spot to go to that becomes your special place. All of this takes time. A community that feels comfortable takes time, but once you know how, you can create and build it wherever you go.

—contributed by Esther Louie

Go now and live

Experience. Dream. Risk. Close your eyes and jump. Enjoy the free fall. Choose exhilaration over comfort. Choose magic over predictability. Choose potential over safety.

Wake up to the magic of everyday life. Make friends with your intuition. Trust your gut. Discover the beauty of uncertainty. Know yourself fully before you make promises to another.

Make millions of mistakes so that you will know how to choose what you really need. Know when to hold on and when to let go. Love hard and often and without reservation.

Seek knowledge. Open yourself to possibility. Keep your heart open, your head high, and your spirit free. Embrace your darkness along with your light. Be wrong every once in a while, and don't be afraid to admit it. Awaken to the brilliance in ordinary moments.

Tell the truth about yourself no matter what the cost. Own your reality without apology. See goodness in the world. Be Bold. Be Fierce. Be Grateful. Be Wild, Crazy, and Gloriously Free. Be You.

Go now, and live.

—contributed by Jeannette LeBlanc

—contributed by Hollis G. Fouts

—contributed by Juita Jayaram

Instructions for using this book:

1. Open to any page.

2. Tear that page out and viciously shred it until you have enough confetti to fill at least one hand, preferably two.

3. Hurl the confetti into the air and whisper to yourself, as it swirls around you in a sweet tornado of chaos, *I am free. My life is my own. It is all, entirely, up to me.*

—*contributed by Siona van Dijk*

—contributed by Patricia Tinsman-Schaffer

It's in your hands

When I was eighteen, I drove with my parents to Guilford College, a campus two hours away from home, and they left me there. In the first or second week of classes, I vividly remember standing outside Binford Dorm looking for speakers on the corners of the buildings or up on the light poles. Finding none, I couldn't figure out how all the announcements would be made.

Remember high school, when the first few minutes of each day were spent listening to the principal making announcements about club meetings and pep rallies? I wondered for quite some time about who would make these announcements at college, and when, and from where could I hear them?

And then I realized that no one was making announcements, that if I wanted to join the Ecology Club or yearbook staff, I'd need to make the effort, find out, track down the information myself. The realization was a big one. It was in my hands, to echo Eliav Zakay's beautiful story from chapter 6.

In just the same way, your life is in your hands.

My friend Nina McIntosh died as the essays that would make up this book were flooding into my e-mail inbox. Nina had ALS, also known as Lou Gehrig's disease, and had chosen me as one of her caregivers in that final year of her life because, as she said, she liked my calm energy and the fact that I didn't look at her with a sad face when I visited. If there is a more horrible disease than ALS, please don't tell me about it right now. Together we navigated her loss of walking, standing, speaking, chewing, and—finally—breathing. And though Nina knew she was eventually going to die from ALS, the end was swifter than any of us ever imagined.

Just a few weeks before she died, I asked her the question behind this collection of essays, thinking that her teetering so closely to the edge of dying and having watched so much of life be haikued to a single breath would imbue her answer with some great vision and knowledge and wisdom that the rest of us can't yet see.

Having already lost the ability to speak, Nina immediately took the yellow legal pad she kept nearby and scratched out her answer, holding the paper out for me to take.

I looked down. "Just remember to change your oil" was all she had written. I looked up to catch a smile, ever so faintly, cross her face.

I handed back the pad of paper and she wrote the rest of the story. Someone had offered her advice as a high school senior, she wrote, and the only thing she remembered from all they told her was to change her oil.

Be you.

Be passionate.

Be present.

Be unsure.

Be curious.

Be free.

And just remember to change your oil.

—*contributed by Sherry Smyth*

Artists & writers

The following creative people have kindly contributed their work for inclusion in this book. Copyright remains with the contributor.

Kathryn Antyr, www.truenortharts.com; **Tamara** Bailie; **Robert C.** Ballard; **Elizabeth D.** Beck, http://ebeckartist.blogspot.com; **Linda** Bannan; **Kerrie** Blazek, www.kerrieblazek.com; **Patti** Bourne, http://wtmu.blogspot.com; **Grace** Bower, www.wisetolife.com; **Lisa** Call, www.lisacall.com; **Mary** Campbell, www.marycampbelldesign.com; **Cynthia N.** Clack, http://alifeprofound.wordpress.com; **Linda** Clearwater, www.lindaclearwater.com; **Jodi** Cohen, www.jodi-cohen.com; **Wendy** Cook, www.wendycook.com; **Debbi** Crane, http://the-art-lady.blogspot.com; **Monica K.** Dahl; **Mary** Davies; **Ruth M.** Davis; **Sarah** Davis, Bristol, ME; **R.L.** Delight, http://RDL-artequalslife.blogspot.com; **Elizabeth** Derrico; **Michelle** Drabik, http://madmusingsblog.blogspot.com; **Betsy L.** Edwards; **Lisa** Evans, www.beachdance.com; **Lie** Fhung, http://liefhung.com; **Hollis G.** Fouts; **Rina** Yuriko Francisco. www.flickr.com/photos/rinayuriko; **Elizabeth** Funkey; **Julie** Galante, www.juliegalante.com; **Louise** Gale, www.louisegale.com; **Lori** Gillen; **Allison** Graham; **Jolie** Guillebeau, www.jolieguillebeau.com; **Renee** Haas, www.reneehaas.com; **Erika** Harris, www.lifeblazing.com; **Tracy L.** Hart, http://unfoldingmoment.blogspot.com; **Teresa** Hartley; **Thomai** Hatsios, http://thomai-in-la.blogspot.com; **Joy** Holland, http://unfoldingyourpathtojoy.wordpress.com; **Jennifer L.** Cohen Incorvaia, www.jivemonkeyproductions.com; **Juita** Jayaram, www.skribblejots.blogspot.com; **Heloise** Jones; **Kimberly** Joris, www.thefolksart.com; **Gabrielle** Kaasa, http://blog.nutellaisevil.net; **Liz** Kettle, www.textileevolution.com; **Cathy** Kirwan, www.tinniegirl.com.au; **Leah** Piken Kolidas, http://BlueTreeArtGallery.com, http://CreativeEveryDay.com; **Felecia** Krech; **Jane** LaFazio, www.PlainJaneStudio.com, http://www.janeville.blogspot.com; **Jeannette** LeBlanc, http://jeanetteleblanc.com, http://www.peacelovefree.com,

http://awakeningsblog.com; **Wendee** Higa Lee; **Kelly** J. Letky, www
.mrsmediocrity.com; **Elizabeth** Lombardo, PhD, www.ahappyyou
.com; **Esther** Louie; **Sarah** Love; **Marilyn** Maciel, http://marilyn
.typepad.com/tongueandgroove; **Kim** Mailhot, www.queen-of-arts
.blogspot.com; **Amy** D. McCracken, http://onepersoneveryday.blogspot
.com; **Dian** K. McCray, www.dianmccray.com; Kate McGovern,
www.katemcgovernphoto.com; **Viv** McWaters, www.vivmcwaters
.com.au; **Susan** R. Meisinger; **Gwyn** Michael, www.gwynmichael
.com; **Fiona** Monk, www.wildhorsecoaching.co.uk; **Rebecca** E.
Parsons, www.cre8tivecompass.com/blog; **Jill** Osler; **Rebeca** Price;
John Ptak, http://historyofideasblog.com; **Denita** L. Purser; **Jeremy**
Reynolds; **Susie** Riley, www.orangeswing.com; **David** Robinson, www
.davidrobinsoncreative.com; **Maxine** Rothman, www.knittingbudda
.com; **Carol** A. Sanders; **Kathryn** Ruth Schuth; Eric M. Scott, www
.journalfodderjunkies.com; **Brandie** Sellers, www.simplelifeyoga.com;
Chi Sherman, chisherman.net; **Mahima** Shrestha; **Stacey** Beth Shulman,
www.curvyyogini.com; **Carol** Sloan, www.carolbsloan.blogspot.com;
Lisa K. Smith; **Sherry** Smyth, http://everydaypossibilities.blogspot.com;
Karl Stephan; **Laura** Stinson, www.katzenjammy.com; **Feithline** Stuart,
http://spiritscast.com; **Celeste** Tibbets; **Patricia** Tinsman-Schaffer;
Ije Ude, www.soulpoweredsolutions.com; **Amy** Ludwig VanDerwater,
www.poemfarm.blogspot.com; **Siona** van Dijk, www.sionavandijk
.com; **Mike** Wagner, www.michaelwagner.com; **Deb** Walsh, www
.onecoolfreeidea.com; **Patricia** L. Watson; **Margaret** Williams; **Gloria**
Wooldridge, PEI Canada; Rabbi **Julie** Wolkoff, http://fabricfiber.word
press.com; **Jaime** Wurth, www.consequencefree.net; **Eliav** Zakay

Gratitudes

I have the best blog readers in the world. My thanks to them for joining me on this journey toward more mindful living since 2005 when I began *37days.com,* and particularly to all those who responded recently to my question, "What would you like to tell your 17-year-old self?" Thirty-seven of these are featured in this book, with my thanks to everyone who contributed their thoughts and dreams. My gratitude also runs deep for the artists who have answered the call in this and my last three books, to create their visions of these words. In so doing they have made all these projects so much more like a work of art than a book.

To all the people who teach me daily (hourly) what matters, my thanks. There are too many of you to name; I hope you know who you are. I believe you likely do.

A special thanks to these recent teachers of mine: Kathryn Ruth Schuth, Amy McCracken, Howard Holden, Kurt Reineking, Nagesh Rao, Eliav Zakay, Sid Jordan, Nina McIntosh, my friends in Hastings, Nebraska, and, always, David Robinson.

With thanks to skirt! books and my editor, Mary Norris, for continuing to indulge my desire to write some things down and leave them behind.

And, as always and even more than ever before, to my human survival units—John, Emma, and Tess Ptak—my deepest ever love and recognition that while I'm offering advice to my children for their consideration, they are actually my best teachers. And, of course, to Sim Sim who is still in my lap, purring, after all these books we've written in close proximity.

—*contributed by Tracy L. Hart*

About the author

"If the Buddha had two kids, a dog named Blue, a Southern accent, and a huge crush on Johnny Depp, his name would be Patti Digh," wrote one reviewer after Digh's grassroots bestseller, *Life Is a Verb,* was published. Patti is a Southern-born master storyteller whose stories are full of humor, poignancy, surprise, pain, and knowing. *Life Is a Verb: 37 Days to Wake Up, Be Mindful, and Live Intentionally,* was one of five finalists for the prestigious Books for a Better Life award and a nominee for a Book of the Year award from the Southern Independent Booksellers Association. Her award-winning blog on which it was based, *37days.com,* brings together readers from ages 12 through 95 across the globe. Patti is also the author of *Four-Word Self-Help: Simple Wisdom for Complex Lives* and *Creative Is a Verb: If You're Alive, You're Creative.* Patti and her family live in Asheville, North Carolina. She speaks all over the world about living mindfully, is rather fond of peonies, zinnias, and kindness, writes a thank-you note every morning, and requires laughter in her life on a daily basis.

© *Michael Mauney*

Be in touch, okay?
patti@pattidigh.com
twitter: @pattidigh / facebook: tinyurl.com/pattidighpage
www.37days.com / www.pattidigh.com
Patti Digh, P.O. Box 18323, Asheville, NC 28814 USA